Sprint Car
RACING

By Tom Glave

SportsZone

An Imprint of Abdo Publishing
www.abdopublishing.com

www.abdopublishing.com

Published by Abdo Publishing, a division of ABDO, PO Box 398166, Minneapolis, Minnesota 55439. Copyright © 2015 by Abdo Consulting Group, Inc. International copyrights reserved in all countries. No part of this book may be reproduced in any form without written permission from the publisher. SportsZone™ is a trademark and logo of Abdo Publishing.

Printed in the United States of America, North Mankato, Minnesota
032014
092014

THIS BOOK CONTAINS
RECYCLED MATERIALS

Cover Photo: Shelia Pezer/Cal Sport Media
Interior Photos: Shelia Pezer/Cal Sport Media, 1; John Raoux/AP Images, 4, 45; RacingOne/Getty Images, 7, 12, 18; Action Sports Photography/Shutterstock Images, 9; Christopher Halloran/Shutterstock Images, 11; Source Interlink Media/Getty Images, 14; Justin Hayworth-The Des Moines Register/AP Images, 16; Miles Chrisinger/Icon SMI, 20, 22; John J. Klaiber Jr./Shutterstock Images, 25, 26, 28–29, 34; Bob Harmeyer/Getty Images, 30; Al Behrman/AP Images, 33; Jason Halley-The Chico Enterprise-Record/AP Images, 37; Charlie Neibergall/AP Images, 38, 41; David Allio/Icon SMI, 43

Editor: Patrick Donnelly
Series Designer: Craig Hinton

Library of Congress Control Number: 2014932861

Cataloging-in-Publication Data
Glave, Tom.
 Sprint car racing / Tom Glave.
  p. cm. -- (Inside the speedway)
Includes bibliographical references and index.
ISBN 978-1-62403-407-7
1. Automobile racing--Juvenile literature. 2. Sprint cars--Juvenile literature.   I. Title.
796.72--dc23

                                                           2014932861

TABLE OF CONTENTS

chapter 1

THE GREATEST SHOW ON DIRT

Tony Stewart was on his way to another win. By 2013, he had won the NASCAR Sprint Cup Series three times. Stewart also had won an Indy Racing League (IRL) IndyCar title. Those are two of the biggest racing series in the world.

Yet this 2013 race was in a sprint car on a dirt track in Iowa. Stewart likes to drive the small and powerful sprint cars during breaks in his NASCAR schedule.

Star driver Tony Stewart enjoys racing sprint cars when he has a break from his NASCAR schedule.

He was in first place when a lapped car spun out in front of him. The other car kicked up a cloud of dust. Stewart could not see. He kept driving as fast as he could. He hoped to miss the other car.

Instead, he was headed right for the other car. It was too late to dodge it. The cars crashed at full speed. Stewart's car flipped several times.

Stewart broke his leg in the crash. He had to miss the rest of the 2013 NASCAR season.

Because racing sprint cars is so dangerous, people often ask him why he still does it. Few drivers who have won NASCAR and IndyCar titles would take that risk.

"My answer is always the same: I'm a race driver," he said. "I drive race cars. Stock cars and IndyCars aren't the only race cars on earth. Racing was never just a job for me. It was the thing I loved to do most."

Sprint car racing has come a long way since these drivers battled it out at the Reading Fairgrounds Speedway in Pennsylvania in 1935.

Sprint car racing is a passion that has been around almost as long as the automobile in the United States. It is one of the oldest forms of auto racing in the country. It started when state and county fairgrounds hosted car races in the early 1900s.

The cars have changed a lot over the years, but sprint car racing remains the same. Small cars with big powerful engines race around dirt ovals. Racers glide through muddy turns

Stepping-stone

Many successful IndyCar and NASCAR drivers first drove sprint cars. A. J. Foyt won the United States Auto Club (USAC) sprint car championship in 1960. He won his first Indianapolis 500 a year later. The Indianapolis 500 is one of the world's most famous IndyCar races. Mario Andretti finished third in the USAC point standings in 1964. He won his first IndyCar national championship a year later. Jeff Gordon raced sprint cars as a teenager. He won championships at Bloomington Speedway and Eldora Speedway. Today he is one of NASCAR's biggest stars. Tony Stewart is a big NASCAR star too. He was named USAC's Sprint Car Rookie of the Year in 1991. He won the USAC Sprint Car championship in 1995. That year he also became the first driver to win the Sprint, Midget, and Silver Crown championships in the same year.

before speeding toward the finish line. Crashes send the little cars with funny-looking wings flipping through the air.

Most sprint car races are held on dirt or clay ovals. That is why sprint car racing is called "the greatest show on dirt."

Stewart still remembers the first time he drove a sprint car. "The biggest single thing I remember was feeling, for the first time ever, the brute horsepower," Stewart said. "I just couldn't believe how fast that thing wanted to go on the straightaways."

Sprint cars have the highest power-to-weight ratio of all race cars. This means the cars are light and have powerful 900-horsepower engines. The powerful vehicles can go more than 140 miles per hour (205 kilometers per hour).

Drivers race these small but powerful beasts on short tracks all over the country. Three main groups sanction the races and award points to determine yearly champions. The USAC has hosted sprint car championships since 1956. Today the USAC hosts several different series across the country and the AMSOIL Sprint Car National Championship Series.

The American Sprint Car Series (ASCS) also sponsors several regional series. The ASCS National Sprint Car series awards the Lucas Oil ASCS National Championship to the top driver. The World of Outlaws hosts races in 23 states. The series uses dirt tracks that are between one-quarter and five-eighths of a mile (0.4 and 1.0 km).

Racers compete in the USAC Copper on Dirt race at the Manzanita Speedway in Phoenix, Arizona, in 2009.

A typical sprint car race includes multiple heats. These are short races, sometimes no longer than eight laps, that determine who will race in the finals. The final race determines the overall winner of the event. It can last 25 to 40 laps, depending on the size of the track.

chapter 2

FAIRGROUNDS AND OUTLAWS

Sprint car racing in the United States traces back to the early 1900s. Open-cockpit, open-wheel races sprung up around the country. Those races were held at half-mile and one-mile (0.8 and 1.6 km) dirt tracks at fairgrounds. These dirt tracks were built for horse racing.

Early drivers modified, or cut down, Model T Fords to make the small race cars. The race cars were made to fit only

Sprint car drivers race around a track at the Lakewood Speedway in Atlanta, Georgia, in the 1940s.

Drivers and crew await the start of the Sprint Car races at Gardena Speedway in California in 1957.

the driver. They had streamlined fronts and tails. The open wheels stuck out on each side. They were called Big Cars after Midget auto racing became popular. Midgets are the smallest race cars.

The American Automobile Association (AAA) began sanctioning the events. It developed sets of rules that limited the size of the cars and their engines. But some state fair managers did not want to pay to race with the AAA. They formed the International Motor Contest Association in 1915 to sanction their own races.

The sport gained popularity after World War I (1914–1918). Soon many short tracks were being built just for race cars.

Several different organizations got into sprint car racing in the years that followed. The AAA started its own sprint car series in the 1930s. The USAC was formed in 1955 and began sponsoring sprint car races. The USAC also ran the Indianapolis 500 between 1956 and 1997.

Races outside of the USAC schedule were often unorganized and confusing to fans. Drivers generally went to the track that paid the most. The USAC called drivers who raced outside of its organization "outlaws."

That led Ted Johnson to form the World of Outlaws in 1978. He created the schedule, a set of rules, and a points

2010
A-MAIN CHAMPION
Knoxville, Iowa

system. The World of Outlaws schedule helped the sport grow in popularity because it was more organized than the other series.

The World of Outlaws race on some of the country's most famous dirt tracks. The Knoxville Raceway in Knoxville, Iowa, opened in 1954. The half-mile (0.8 km) raceway hosts the Knoxville Nationals every year. Knoxville is also home to the National Sprint Car Hall of Fame and Museum.

The Eldora Speedway in Rossburg, Ohio, is a half-mile (0.8 km) clay oval that opened in 1954. The Dirt Track at Charlotte Motor Speedway in

Sprint Car's Super Bowl

The Knoxville Nationals is one of sprint car racing's biggest events. In the late 1800s, a horse racing track was built at the Marion County Fairgrounds in Tennessee. The county fair hosted its first car race in 1914.

The Knoxville Raceway started hosting weekly car races in 1954. The Knoxville Nationals were created in 1961 as a championship race for Super Modifieds. It changed to a sprint car race in 1968.

Buzz Barton prepares to race his sprint car in Tampa, Florida, in 1961.

North Carolina hosts the World of Outlaws World Finals at the
end of the season.

Over the years, the race cars on those tracks have changed
as drivers tried to go faster. Different classes of sprint cars also

emerged. Faster engines were introduced in the 1940s and again in the 1960s.

Super Modifieds are another type of sprint car. They evolved from stock cars. The changes made to the stock cars allowed those cars to go faster. The safety roll cage is one feature that both stock cars and Super Modifieds have. Drivers combined the features of Big Cars and Super Modifieds in the late 1960s. These looked like today's sprint cars.

chapter 3

DRIVING A ROLLER COASTER

Sprint cars bounce. They spin. They fly around corners at high speeds. They can make a driver dizzy. Driving them is like riding a roller coaster.

Sprint cars are simple and powerful. Sometimes they look funny because of their size and shape. If a part is not necessary to make the car work, it is not used. This makes them as light as possible.

Sprint cars are simple vehicles that are built for power.

There's not a lot of room for drivers to move around inside the cockpit of a sprint car.

Sprint cars weigh approximately 1,200 pounds (544 kg). They can cost as much as $60,000 to build. A sprint car has a frame made of lightweight steel tubing. The body of the car is only big enough to fit the most important parts. Those parts are the engine, the driver, and the fuel tank. The frame, called a chassis, is about 84 inches (213 cm) long when measured from wheel to wheel. For comparison, a NASCAR race car has a wheelbase of around 110 inches (279 cm).

The sprint car driver sits in the cockpit. It is a small space. The seat is upright. The driver has limited movement after putting on the safety harness. The driver can only see straight ahead.

The steering wheel comes off to make it easier to get in and out of the race car. The dashboard has limited gauges and controls. That keeps the build of the car as simple as possible.

The driveshaft connects the engine to the rear of the race car. The engine sits in front of the driver. The driveshaft runs between the driver's legs. It sits inside a protective tube.

Sprint cars are small, but they are powered by eight-cylinder engines. Engines that size are usually found in much larger vehicles. The extra power they provide helps make the cars go faster.

Race cars in the World of Outlaws and the USAC use 6.7-liter (410-cubic-inch) engines. The ASCS allows only 5.9-liter (360-cubic-inch) engines. Larger engines help cars drive faster.

A sprint car does not use a battery to start the engine. The car needs to be pushed by a truck. As the engine turns, it builds oil pressure. The driver then hits an ignition switch to fire the engine.

Most sprint cars use methanol gas. Methanol is more efficient and safer to use than gasoline. The fuel tank is in the back of the car.

Sprint car races are short. They range from a handful of laps in a heat to 40 laps in a finals race. Drivers do not need to stop during the race to get more gas. The race car can be fitted with different size tanks. Longer races require a bigger fuel tank.

The front and rear wings on a sprint car catch the air around the vehicle to provide downforce, which keeps the car on the track while it makes turns.

Sprint cars use three different size tires. This makes the cars look funny, but the tires are important. The two front tires are the same size. The left rear tire is wider. The right rear tire is taller and wider than the left one. This helps the cars turn left around curves.

Some sprint cars have wings on top. The wings work like upside-down airplane wings. While air pushes an airplane up, here the air pushes the race cars down. This helps the race car turn corners.

The wings help drivers stay in control of their cars. This prevents crashes. If a car crashes, the wings can absorb some of the impact. The wings also give drivers a place to sell advertising.

The World of Outlaws and the ASCS only use winged race cars. The USAC does not allow wings.

Wings Take Flight

Ohio race car driver Jim Cushman used the first aerodynamic wing in 1958. Cushman started winning because of the advantage from the wing. Cushman tested the idea by using plywood on top of his pickup truck. He tested different angles before mounting a wing to his race car. Other drivers copied the wing. The use of wings spread from there.

SPRINT CAR Photo Diagram

1. **NOSE WING:** This keeps the front of the car in balance. A nose wing is typically no more than six square feet (.55 m²).

2. **REAR WING:** It creates downforce to help with traction. Typically a rear wing is five feet by five feet (1.5 m x 1.5 m).

3. **CHASSIS:** Built from lightweight steel tubing, chassis are similar in most sprint cars.

4. **REAR TIRES:** Wider than front tires, they help keep the car stable through turns.

5. **FRONT TIRES:** All sprint car tires are designed with soft sidewalls to give the driver more traction and control.

6. **COCKPIT:** The driver is strapped in here with a five-point harness for safety purposes.

7. **ENGINE:** It has eight cylinders to provide extra power for the small car.

1

5

chapter 4

LEARNING ON THE FLY

Doug Wolfgang won more than 100 sprint car races during his career. He won the Knoxville Nationals five times. He is now a member of the National Sprint Car Hall of Fame.

Wolfgang paid for his first race car. He bought one that had crashed. He did not know much about racing yet. First he learned how to fix the car. Then he learned how to race the car.

Doug Wolfgang is a five-time Knoxville Nationals winner who was inducted into the National Sprint Car Hall of Fame in 2003.

"The more I learned, the more I enjoyed it," Wolfgang said. "The more I enjoyed it, the better I became."

Wolfgang said it is not hard to make sprint cars go fast. They are made to go fast. The hard part is learning to make the sprint cars perform their best. Drivers need to know how to make adjustments based on track conditions.

They learn how to make these adjustments through experience. Veteran drivers know their race cars and the tracks very well. Most sprint car races are on dirt. The tracks come in many different sizes. A wet dirt track is different to drive on than a dry dirt track.

Drivers have to adjust their car to drive on the different tracks. Sprint cars use different tires for different track conditions. Groove

Still Involved

NASCAR champion Tony Stewart formed Tony Stewart Racing in 2000. He now owns five sprint car teams. His teams race in the World of Outlaws and the USAC series.

The World of Outlaws title in 2001 was his team's first championship. Stewart's teams have won eight USAC titles and four World of Outlaws titles through 2013. Stewart also owns the Eldora Speedway in Rossburg, Ohio.

NASCAR champion Tony Stewart remains heavily involved in sprint car racing. He owns five sprint car teams and the Eldora Speedway in Rossburg, Ohio.

patterns on a tire's surface will determine how much grip it provides. Drivers want more grip on a slippery track. Drivers also can move the wing. The wing is pushed back when the track is slick. This gives the back tires more traction. They grip the ground better. The wing can be closer to the front when the track is sticky. This gives the front tires more traction.

Sprint cars slide through turns on the rough terrain of dirt tracks.

The speedy sprint cars skid around the curves of the racetrack. Drivers need to learn how to slide quickly through the turns. Doing that lets them straighten the car and pick up speed on the straightaway. However, some sprint car races are on pavement. Race cars cannot slide around curves on pavement the same way.

People drive normal cars with one foot. They move their right foot from the gas pedal to the brake. Sprint car drivers use both feet to drive. The right foot pushes the throttle. That is the gas pedal that makes the race car go. The left foot pushes the brake pedal. The right foot cannot reach the brake pedal because the driveshaft tube is in the way.

Drivers have to get used to the car's small cockpit. Once they get seated, they can only move their arms and legs. This helps keep them safe.

The loud engines create a lot of noise. Drivers cannot hear what is going on around them. They also cannot turn their heads. They must focus on what they can see in front of them. They watch for race cars that have crashed. They keep an eye on track conditions. They look for the best path around each curve.

Most sprint car races last about 30 minutes. They do not have pit stops like longer races. Drivers also do not sit in their race cars for long periods of time. The race is over quickly and the drivers move on to their next event. Sprint car drivers have a busy schedule. They can race several times a week in different cities.

chapter 5

THE KING AND HIS COURT

Steve Kinser knew from an early age he wanted to race cars. He learned a lot about racing by watching his father, Bob, race. The younger Kinser started racing go-karts and motorcycles when he was 11 years old. His love for competition was clear from the start too. He was a state champion wrestler in high school.

Kinser started racing sprint cars at age 22. He joined the World of Outlaws series when

Steve Kinser has had plenty of opportunities to celebrate as one of the greatest sprint car racers of all time.

it was formed in 1978. Kinser won his first World of Outlaws race at Eldora Speedway in May 1978.

He won the very first World of Outlaws championship in 1978. That was the start of his record-setting career. Kinser won the first three World of Outlaws season championships. That success earned him the nickname "King of the Outlaws."

Through 2013 Kinser had won the World of Outlaws championship 20 times. He won 11 World of Outlaws championships in a 12-year period between 1983 and 1994. He had won 576 World of Outlaws races and more than 800 sprint car races in his career. That was the most of any driver.

All in the Family

The Kinser family is one of the most famous in sprint car racing. Bob Kinser won more than 400 sprint car races during his career. He was inducted into the National Sprint Car Hall of Fame in 1999. His son Steve Kinser is also in the Hall of Fame. He has more victories than any other sprint car driver.

Steve Kinser's son Kraig is also a driver. He won the World of Outlaws Rookie of the Year award in 2004. Steve's daughter, Stevie, and his wife, Dana, help run the family racing team.

Donny Schatz became the face of sprint car racing by winning five World of Outlaws championships in eight years.

Kinser also competed in other auto racing series. He was invited to race in the International Race of Champions several times. That is a type of all-star competition. It pits racers from a variety of disciplines against each other in identical cars. Kinser tried the NASCAR circuit in 1995, and he raced the Indianapolis 500 in 1997.

Kinser won his twentieth World of Outlaws season title in 2005. Donny Schatz has dominated the series since then.

Schatz also started racing go-karts at age 11. By 15 he had moved to sprint cars. He won the World of Outlaws Rookie of the Year award in 1997 at age 20.

Schatz won his first Knoxville Nationals in 2006. He also won his first World of Outlaws championship that year. Between 2006 and 2013 he won five World of Outlaws championships and finished in second place three times. He also has won the Knoxville Nationals seven times. That is second only to Kinser's 20 titles.

The USAC has its share of stars too. Bryan Clauson started racing sprint cars in 2003. He won six races in 2004 at age 14. He started racing in the USAC after his sixteenth birthday.

Bryan Clauson was a teenage race star who went on to win the National Sprint Car championship in 2012 and 2013.

In 2013 he became the eighth driver in USAC history to win two straight National Sprint Car championships.

Levi Jones won five USAC titles between 2005 and 2011. He won his third straight championship in 2011. He was the third driver in history to win three in a row.

USAC sponsors championships in three divisions. Midget cars are smaller than sprint cars, and Silver Crown are a little bigger. J. J. Yeley won the championship in all three divisions in 2003. That's called the Triple Crown. He was the second driver to win it. Yeley also raced in the Indianapolis 500 in 1998. He started racing in the NASCAR series in 2004.

GLOSSARY

ADJUSTMENT
The act or process of changing or fixing something.

AERODYNAMICS
How air flowing around a car can affect its speed and handling.

CHASSIS
The frame of a car.

FAIRGROUNDS
An area set aside for fairs, circuses, and exhibitions. Many sprint car racetracks are at fairgrounds.

SANCTION
To oversee and regulate something.

STOCK CAR
A standard car that is modified for racing.

STREAMLINE
To improve the outline or design of a car to make it more aerodynamic.

THROTTLE
A valve that controls the flow of steam or fuel to an engine.

TRACTION
The grip that allows a tire to stay on the ground.

WHEELBASE
The distance between the front and rear axles of a motor vehicle.

FOR MORE INFORMATION

Further Readings

Hantula, Richard. *Science at Work in Auto Racing*. New York: Marshall Cavendish Benchmark, 2012.

Scheff, Matt. *Tony Stewart*. Minneapolis, MN: Abdo Publishing Company, 2013.

Von Finn, Denny. *Sprint Cars*. Minneapolis, MN: Bellwether Media, Inc., 2009.

Wolfgang, Doug. *Lone Wolf: One of Auto Racing's Most Compelling Characters Tells His Story*. Fishers, IN: American Scene Press, 2007.

Websites

To learn more about Inside the Speedway, visit **booklinks.abdopublishing.com**. These links are routinely monitored and updated to provide the most current information available.

INDEX

About the Author

Tom Glave has covered prep and college sports for newspapers in New Jersey, Missouri, Arkansas, and Texas. He won multiple awards from the Arkansas Press Association during a seven-year stay at *The Benton County Daily Record*. He lives in the Houston area with his wife and two sons.